Learn About

ANIMAL COVERINGS

MW01139244

SHELLS

by Eric Geron

Children's Press®
An imprint of Scholastic Inc.

Library of Congress Cataloging-in-Publication Data

Names: Geron, Eric, author.
Title: Shells / by Eric Geron.
Description: First edition. | New York : Children's Press, an imprint of
   Scholastic Inc., 2024. | Series: Learn about: animal coverings |
   Includes index. | Audience: Ages 5–7 | Audience: Grades K–1 | Summary:
   "Let's learn all about the different types of animal coverings! Animals
   have different body coverings for different reasons. Some animals use
   their coverings to keep warm or stay cool, others use them for
   protection, and can either stand out or blend in. Some animals even use
   their coverings to move! This vibrant new set of LEARN ABOUT books gives
   readers a close-up look at five different animal coverings, from fur and
   feathers to skin, scales, and shells. Each book is packed with
   photographs and fun facts that explore how each covering suits the
   habitat, diet, survival, and life cycle of various animals in the
   natural world. Armadillos, snails, and turtles are just some of the
   animals that have shells. Do you know why these animals need shells to
   survive? With amazing photos and lively text, this book explains how
   shells help animals move, protect themselves, hide, and more! Get ready
   to learn all about shells!"—Provided by publisher.
Identifiers: LCCN 2023000181 (print) | LCCN 2023000182 (ebook) |
   ISBN 9781338898088 (library binding) | ISBN 9781338898095 (paperback) |
   ISBN 9781338898101 (ebook)
Subjects: LCSH: Shells—Juvenile literature. | Body covering
   (Anatomy)—Juvenile literature. | Animal defenses—Juvenile literature.
   | Animals—Adaptation—Juvenile literature. | BISAC: JUVENILE NONFICTION
   / Animals / General | JUVENILE NONFICTION / Science & Nature / General
   (see also headings under Animals or Technology)
Classification: LCC QL405.2 .G47 2024 (print) | LCC QL405.2 (ebook) |
   DDC 591.47/7—dc23/eng/20230110
LC record available at https://lccn.loc.gov/2023000181
LC ebook record available at https://lccn.loc.gov/2023000182

10 9 8 7 6 5 4 3 2 1   24 25 26 27 28
Printed in China   62

First edition, 2024
Book design by Kay Petronio

Photos ©: cover: Thomas A. Schneider/Alamy Images; 5 main:
real444/Getty Images; 5 inset: Randy Faris/Getty Images; 6–7
background: Alfred Pasieka/Science Photo Library/Getty Images;
7 top right: panda3800/Getty Images; 11 top: mikroman6/Getty
Images; 11 bottom: Joehollins/Bournemouth News/Shutterstock; 13
main: NLBFoto/Getty Images; 15: Marco Cícero Cavallini/EyeEm/
Getty Images; 16 bottom: Giordano Cipriani/Getty Images; 18–19
main: Gerard Soury/Getty Images; 19 inset: Richard McMillin/Getty
Images; 22: Perry Mastrovito/Alamy Images; 24 bottom: Rodger
Shagam/Getty Images; 25: Michel VIARD/Getty Images; 26 bottom:
MassanPH/Getty Images; 28 inset: Jay Fleming/Getty Images; 30 top right:
WestLight/Getty Images.

All other photos © Shutterstock.

A special thank-you
to the team at the
Cincinnati Zoo &
Botanical Garden
for their expert
consultation.

CONTENTS

Special Shells

Animal bodies can have different coverings. Some are covered with skin. Others are covered with fur, feathers, or scales. This book is all about a special covering: shells! Shells can be swirly or striped, pointed or rounded, and thin or wide.

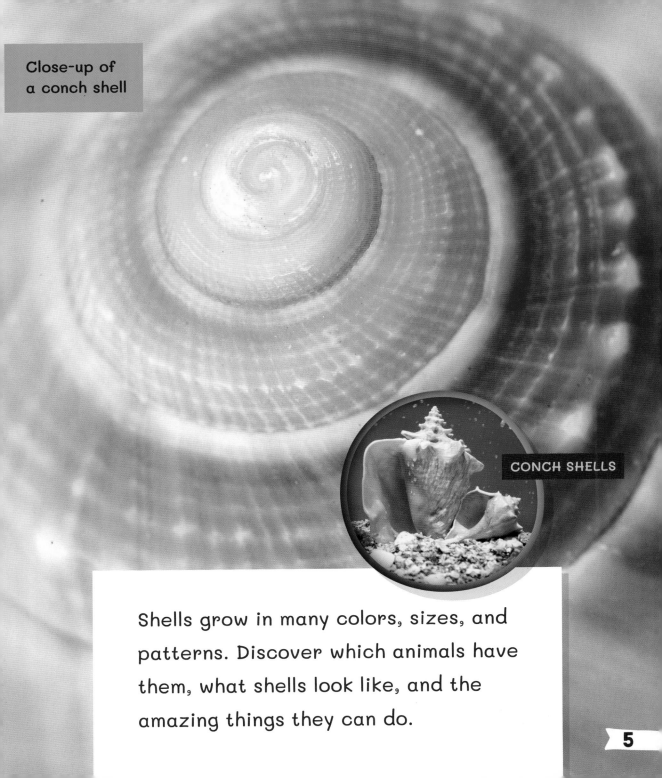

Close-up of
a conch shell

CONCH SHELLS

Shells grow in many colors, sizes, and
patterns. Discover which animals have
them, what shells look like, and the
amazing things they can do.

Which Animals Have Shells?

Mollusks, **crustaceans**, insects, sea urchins, and turtles have shells. Some examples of mollusks are clams, mussels, oysters, snails, and scallops.

Another word for the large shell that covers some animal's bodies is *exoskeleton*.

Some examples of crustaceans are crabs, lobsters, and shrimp. Animals with shells live on land or live in water. Their hard outer shells can all look different.

CHAPTER 1

Shell Help

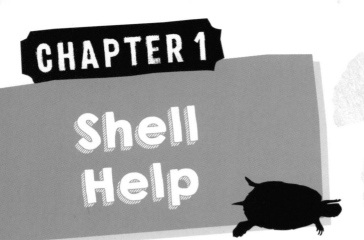

Shells are really useful. Just like there are different types of animals, there are also different types of shells. Each type of shell plays an important role. Some shells help support an animal's body as it moves.

BANDED JEWEL BEETLE

Wind crab inside its shell

ABALONE SHELL

Some shells keep an animal on land from drying out. Sometimes shells help an animal when it is time to feed. Some shells hide an animal from **predators** or **prey**. Some shells can even act like a home!

Did you know that the armadillo is the only *mammal* with a shell?

Shell

This is a snail. It uses its shell to protect its soft body. When danger comes, the snail can hide inside its shell. Many **species** of turtles can also hide inside their shells to avoid danger. Turtle shells come in different shapes and weights.

SNAIL SHELL CLOSE-UP

Most snail shells are in a spiral pattern. They are usually brown, yellow, or white in color.

The shells of sea turtles are lighter in weight and smooth to help them glide through the water. The shells of tortoises are heavy and bumpy to keep them safe from predators.

SEA TURTLE

SEYCHELLES GIANT TORTOISE

CHAPTER 2

Saved by the Shell

Shells protect animals in other ways. Without a shell, an animal can get injured more easily or eaten! Predators have a hard time breaking open the shells and sometimes give up trying.

Sea otters use rocks to break open the shells of mollusks and sea urchins for a tasty snack.

Seagull trying to eat a crab

SEA URCHIN

Sea urchins have prickly shells that make predators not want to eat them.

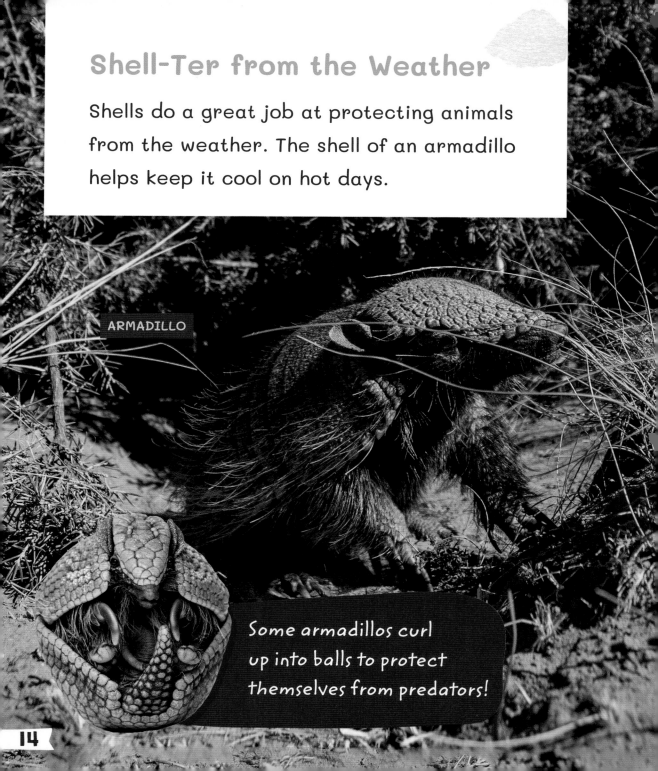

Shell-Ter from the Weather

Shells do a great job at protecting animals from the weather. The shell of an armadillo helps keep it cool on hot days.

ARMADILLO

Some armadillos curl up into balls to protect themselves from predators!

DESERT SNAIL

The shell of a desert snail reflects sunlight to protect it from the heat. The shell of a sea urchin protects it like a shield from harsh cold at the bottom of the sea.

CHAPTER 3

Hide-and-Go-Shell

Many animals have shells that let them hide in their **habitat**. The ability to blend into their surroundings is called **camouflage**. Camouflage helps protect animals from being seen by predators or prey.

Did you know that lobsters' shells help them camouflage in the ocean and come in many different colors?

SEA TURTLE

GHOST CRAB

The sea turtle disappears into its surroundings. The pattern of its shell looks like sunrays beaming down into the water. A young ghost crab can look exactly like the sandy seafloor.

Shell Decoration

Some animals with shells can camouflage by putting things on top of them. The sea urchin gathers rocks and shells on the seafloor and is able to disguise itself.

SEA URCHIN

DECORATOR CRAB

YELLOW-BELLIED SLIDER TURTLES

The decorator crab puts sponges and seaweed on its shell to blend in with its habitat. **Algae** on turtle shells and crab shells make them seem like part of the scenery.

CHAPTER 4

Shed or Grow

All crustaceans lose their shells and replace them with new ones. This is called **molting**, or shedding. As the crustacean grows, it molts its shell for a bigger one. This way the shell can grow with the rest of the body.

If a lobster is missing body parts, it can regrow them when it molts!

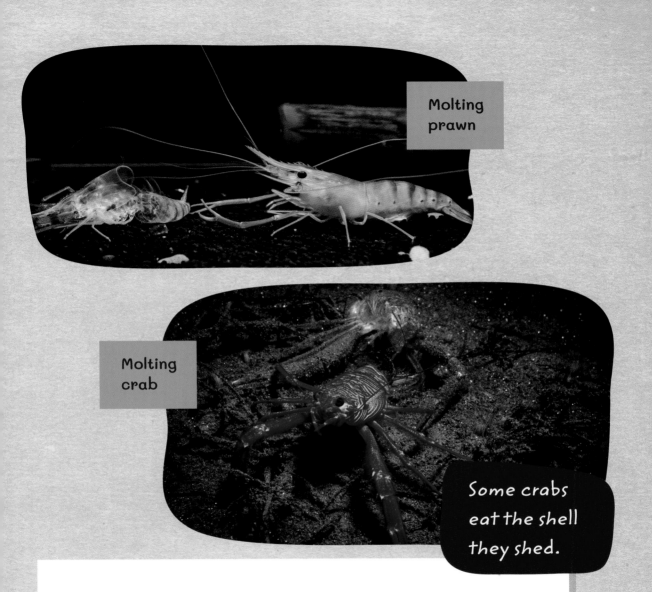

Molting prawn

Molting crab

Some crabs eat the shell they shed.

The new shell starts off soft and then hardens once the crustacean grows into its new size. Shedding is a good way to get rid of any pests sticking to the old shell.

All turtles molt their shells. The thin pieces of shell that turtles molt are called scutes.

Molting painted turtle

Mollusks, such as clams, and armadillos do not shed their shells. Their shells grow larger over time along with the rest of the body.

CLAMS

CHAPTER 5

What Else Can Shells Do?

Shells can also protect eggs. Many animals, such as birds and some reptiles, lay eggs with shells.

BLACKSMITH PLOVER EGGS

Some eggshells camouflage into their environments to keep them safe from predators!

Crocodile eggs hatching

The eggs are covered by eggshells. The eggshells keep the baby growing inside safe from things like **bacteria**.

Insect Shells

Believe it or not, insects have shells, too. Insects use their shells for protection and to keep from drying out. Insects also shed their shells as they grow.

LADYBUG

The shield bug is an insect. Its name comes from the shape of its shell.

SHIELD BUG

JEWEL BUG

DUNG BEETLES

Some insects have a shiny coating on their shells. It serves as a warning to predators not to eat them, and to help them camouflage. Some insect shells cover and protect the insect's wings.

Shell Snacks

Many mollusks, like clams, oysters, and scallops, have two shells. These mollusks are called **bivalves**. They open their shells to feed on tiny foods.

SCALLOP

Octopus inside
a clam shell

Some snails feed
on smaller snails.
Turtles will eat
snails, beetles,
and plants.
Crustaceans eat
algae, worms,
smaller shrimp,
and snails, among
other things.

Many animals, such as
fish, crabs, and octopuses,
make their homes inside
abandoned shells.

CONCLUSION

Shells Matter

Now you know all about shells! They can be smooth or bumpy, and soft or hard. Shells come in all colors, shapes, and sizes. Animals need them to survive. Shells help animals defend themselves against danger and keep them from drying out. They also help animals hide from view. Next time you see an animal with a shell, remember how its shell makes so many things possible for it.

The mollusk with the largest shell is the giant clam, with a shell over 4 feet (1 m) wide!

GLOSSARY

algae (AL-jee) small plants without roots or stems that grow mainly in water

bacteria (bak-TEER-ee-uh) any one of a group of very small living things that may cause disease

bivalve (BYE-valv) a mollusk that lives inside two shells that close together

camouflage (KAM-uh-flahzh) a disguise or natural coloring that allows animals to hide by making them look like their surroundings

crustacean (kruh-STAY-shuhn) a spineless animal with a hard body, such as a crab, lobster, or shrimp

exoskeleton (ek-soh-SKEL-uh-tuhn) a supportive covering of an animal

habitat (HAB-i-tat) the place where an animal or plant is usually found

mammal (MAM-uhl) a warm-blooded animal that has hair or fur and usually gives birth to live babies

NAUTILUS SHELL

mollusk (MAH-luhsk) an animal with a soft body, no spine, and usually a hard shell that lives in water or a damp habitat

molt (mohlt) to lose old fur, feathers, shell, or skin so that a new layer can grow

predator (PRED-uh-tur) an animal that lives by hunting other animals for food

prey (pray) an animal that is hunted by another animal for food

species (SPEE-sheez) one of the groups into which animals and plants are divided

INDEX

ABOUT THE AUTHOR

Eric Geron is the author of many books. He lives in New York City with his tiny dog, who once dressed as a turtle for Halloween.